Miracles in the
A 31-Day Adver

Self-Published Copyright © 2020 Stephanie Yttrup
Cover & Interior Design © by
Stephanie LaPreal Creative
www.stephanielapreal.com
All rights reserved.

No part of this publication may be reproduced, stored in a retrieval system or transmitted in any form by any means, electronic, mechanical, photocopy, recording or otherwise, without the prior permission of the publishers except as provided by USA copyright law.

Unless otherwise noted, Scripture quotations marked (ESV®) are taken from the Holy Bible, English Standard Version®, copyright © 2001 by Crossway, a publishing ministry of Good News Publishers. Used by permission. All rights reserved.

Permission to Quote: The ESV text may be quoted (in written, visual, or electronic form) up to and inclusive of one thousand (1,000) verses without express written permission of the publisher, providing that the verses quoted do not amount to a complete book of the Bible nor do the verses quoted account for 50 percent or more of the total text of the work in which they are quoted.

Printed in the United States of America

For the Father who saw me when no one else could have, came down to meet me when my mess was too much, showed me the gift of an abundant life with Him, and has never left my side.

For my family and friends who constantly call out my gifts when I can't even see them myself and remind me to never stop chasing the dreams God puts in front of me. Thanks for loving me, encouraging me, and pushing me closer to Jesus every day.

Miracles in the Meantime

A 31-Day Advent Devotional

By Stephanie LaPreal Yttrup

TABLE OF *Contents*

9   INTRODUCTION
What is Advent?

13   MEETING US IN THE MESSINESS
Days 1 - 5

39   MORE THAN ENOUGH
Days 6 - 13

75   MEANING IN EVERY MOMENT
Days 14 - 20

107   MIRACLES IN THE MEANTIME
Days 21 - 25

131   MOVING INTO GOD'S CALLING
Days 26 - 31

161   ABOUT THE AUTHOR

Introduction to Advent

Over 2,000 years ago, a baby was brought into this world that changed everything forever. He was the One many had waited for. He was the plan all along, but no one really knew what this meant for humanity. What we now know is that it was the new beginning of a world with Jesus in our hearts and here with us forever. We now know that it was the first day of the rest of our lives as redeemed and beloved children of God. We now know that day as Christmas, but Advent is far greater than just a day of remembrance.

Advent literally means the arrival of a notable person or event. Waiting. Advent is the result of waiting, and we all know what waiting seasons can feel like. Often, we don't see the end result in our own timing, and that makes it harder to find meaning while we wait. For Christmas though, we know the ending, and really the end of waiting was just the beginning. But what does that first Christmas all those years ago mean for us *today*? How can the arrival of our Savior bring us love, joy, peace, and hope while we face hard trials?

As I sat on my couch one evening, I glanced up at the wall next to my fireplace. There hung a letter board with a timeless Christmas phrase that I never took down from the prior year.

"A thrill of hope, the weary world rejoices."

My gut reaction in that moment was not peace, hope, love, or joy. It was confusion, fear, and bewilderment. How, in the midst of tense social climates, political warfare, a mental and physical health pandemic, racial injustice, and complete unrest, could our weary world possibly rejoice?! *How big does hope need to be in a world like this to bring such uninhibited joy in the middle of unimaginable trials?* I didn't know, and I gave that confused and fearful burden to God, knowing that He is the ultimate source of a hope that big.

This world is ever-changing; things are great one day and terrible the next. Trends come and go like waves, and it leaves us spinning and depressed if that's all we're focused on. Christmas, or what many in the Christian faith refer to as Advent, is supposed to be a season of remembrance, hope, and peace. So, here you are, wondering how this Advent season could be different, how it could feel fuller and more energizing, how you can re-discover hope and light despite the chaos of everyday life, shopping, parties, tense family gatherings, and stories of Santa Claus coming to town.

Every Advent season, I feel anxious, worried, lost in the hustle, and I come out feeling more empty. December 25th comes, and I'm like a little kid on Christmas morning. I pray, thanking God for sending His son as a precious babe; we celebrate with family, and then turn the page to the next year and just keep moving forward. I never pause. I never stay still. I never reminisce (until it comes time to plan goals for the new year). I am ALWAYS ready for the next best thing, and

I don't sit still long enough to see what God might be trying to show me *in the meantime.*

The waiting is the painful part. Sitting still is uncomfortable. I get restless and feel out of control when I wait without knowing what's next. Heck, I don't like waiting when I DO know what's next! God gently reminds me each year to slow down. December 1st comes around, and I am invited by the Spirit to pause, breathe in the wonder, and allow each day to be filled with ways to draw closer to the Reason for the Season.

So, I invite you into the discomfort, the pain, the laughable joy, and the surrender of Advent. My hope and prayer is that this devotional will be a reminder each day to draw near to the One who drew near to you so many years ago and never left your side. Each day is filled with a Scripture to meditate on, a brief story, and a place to reflect and see God in your midst. Taking a page out of Anne Lamott's book, "Help, **Thanks, Wow."** *you'll see additional space to write out a prayer and talk to God. It can be as simple as "help," "thanks," or "wow."*

So, light a candle, find that cozy spot, and prepare your heart for God to reveal just what you need this season. **Because I know that waiting is messy, but Jesus showed up in the barn of an inn to prove to us that there really can be miracles in the meantime.**

meeting us in the
messiness

JESUS IS
our good news

December 1

We live in a messy world, but thankfully it isn't too messy for our Savior to meet us here.

"And the angel said to them, 'Fear not, I bring you good news of great joy that will be for all the people.'"
Luke 2:10

Let's be honest, there are multiple moments throughout the day when you feel like even Christmas might not do it for you this year. When chaos, frustration, pain or transition swirls around us, it's hard to see "good news of great joy." This devotional is not meant to be full of platitudes and basic holiday greetings that give you that warm fuzzy feeling in December but leave you empty and starving for more in January.

Often we skip to the great joy, but the angel's greeting to the shepherds started with two simple words: "fear not." In order to embrace, remember, and really allow the good news of Christ's birth to transform us to see great joy, we must lay down our fears at the base of the manger. Recognizing that things are not always perfect gives us the space to see the good news for all it's worth, and that's the gospel of grace. So, what do you need to lay down today, friend?

Reflect & Pray

What fear, pain, grief or shame is holding you back from receiving the greatest joy of Jesus' arrival into your heart this Advent season?

Fear of not having a chance to lead, change children's ministry, my voice being accepted

As we begin this journey toward Advent, what kind of good news do you need?

- Love
- Kes' love for Jesus is present

Lord, I pray that you would use the next 31 days of this holiday season to remind us that it's all about You. Remind us of Your goodness. Remind us of Your life on earth that brought us closer to You than ever before. Give us the space to hold Your truth tighter than the burdens this world puts on our shoulders. Show us how only You can redeem the time we've wasted just waiting for the great joy at the end instead of recognizing the miracles in our midst. We give this season to You.

Help. Thanks. Wow.

JESUS IS
the creative creator

December 2

From the beginning, God's plan was focused on goodness and grace.

"God saw all that He had made and it was very good."
Genesis 1:31

To grasp the beauty and awe of the gift of Jesus at Christmastime, it's important to go back to the beginning to remember God's plan for all of it. In the seven days God created the world, He made water, sky, land, plants, birds, fish, mammals, reptiles, and humans—literally everything you see, feel, touch, hear and smell in nature is all because of God's creativity. When He finished creating, He said, "THIS IS VERY GOOD." You. God looked at you and said, "You are very good." He is PROUD of what He created.

Because we serve a triune God, Jesus was there at the beginning too. He was with God at the beginning of time, waiting until His debut on earth to be with us and stay with us through the Holy Spirit. Things got a little messy along the way, though.

> "The Lord God made garments of skin for Adam and his wife and clothed them. And the Lord God said, 'The man has now become like one of us, knowing good and evil. He must not be allowed to reach out his hand and take also from the tree of life and eat, and live forever.'
> So the Lord God banished him from the Garden of

Eden to work the ground from which he had been taken." Genesis 3:21-23

When Adam and Eve sinned, their eyes were opened to good and evil in the world because that was the tree they ate from—the fruit God told them not to eat. If you know the story, you probably remember the banishing, but read the passage one more time.

God recognized the weight of what life would be like for humanity knowing good and evil, facing the sinful nature within us, and having to live forever like that. I don't know about you, but I'm grateful He banished Adam and Eve from an eternity of knowing pain and suffering! Even when things got messy, God had a plan. He knew what was best, and He was ready for the redemptive promise in His Son Jesus that would come many years later.

Reflect & Pray

How does this reminder of how God graciously banished Adam and Eve bring you hope?

God continues his goodness in my mistakes

This Advent, what are your deepest prayers to your Heavenly Father? Write them out on the next page so at the end of the 31 days, you can come back and see how God moved in your heart.

Help. Thanks. Wow.

- Help Dad walk & back healed
- Help continue relationships w/ Kaiden & Katelynn
- Help marriage during busy season
- Help Kes' faith journey

Thank you for pockets of your redemption in Kes
- Thank you for healthcare & insurance
- Thank you for Polar Express
- Thank you for work food working cars clothes insurance

JESUS IS *in the details*

December 3

Our role in the process is to trust.

"This is the genealogy of Jesus the Messiah the son of David, the son of Abraham:
Abraham was the
father of Isaac,
Isaac the father of Jacob,
Jacob the father of Judah and his brothers,
Judah the father of Perez and Zerah, whose mother was Tamar,
Perez the father of Hezron,
Hezron the father of Ram,
Ram the father of Amminadab,
Amminadab the father of Nahshon,
Nahshon the father of Salmon,
Salmon the father of Boaz, whose mother was Rahab,
Boaz the father of Obed, whose mother was Ruth,
Obed the father of Jesse,
and Jesse the father of King David.
David was the father of Solomon, whose mother had been Uriah's wife,
Solomon the father of Rehoboam,
Rehoboam the father of Abijah,
Abijah the father of Asa,
Asa the father of Jehoshaphat,
Jehoshaphat the father of Jehoram,
Jehoram the father of Uzziah,
Uzziah the father of Jotham,
Jotham the father of Ahaz,
Ahaz the father of Hezekiah,

Hezekiah the father of Manasseh,
Manasseh the father of Amon,
Amon the father of Josiah,
and Josiah the father of Jeconiah and his brothers at the time of the exile to Babylon.
After the exile to Babylon:
Jeconiah was the father of Shealtiel,
Shealtiel the father of Zerubbabel,
Zerubbabel the father of Abihud,
Abihud the father of Eliakim,
Eliakim the father of Azor,
Azor the father of Zadok,
Zadok the father of Akim,
Akim the father of Elihud,
Elihud the father of Eleazar,
Eleazar the father of Matthan,
Matthan the father of Jacob,
and Jacob the father of Joseph, the husband of Mary, and Mary was the mother of Jesus who is called the Messiah.
Thus there were fourteen generations in all from Abraham to David, fourteen from David to the exile to Babylon,
and fourteen from the exile to the Messiah."
Matthew 1:1-17

Don't miss this. We all tend to skim over genealogies in the Bible because they feel insignificant, but this one is full of rich promises for the Advent season specifically. This lineage is messy. What names do you recognize? In case you don't know them, here are a few of the stories woven throughout this lineage.

Abraham and Sarah waited a LONG time for their child Isaac, and even though they knew the promise of his coming, they tried to take matters into their own hands.

Judah led the idea with his brothers to sell Joseph into slavery due to their jealousy of him.

Ruth lost her first husband, brothers-in-law, and father-in-law before finding Boaz.

David, the youngest in his family and most unlikely to amount to anything more than a shepherd boy was anointed to be King, and hunted for many years by King Saul. While in command, he slept with a soldier's wife, impregnated her, and put him on the front lines of the war so he would die before finding out the mistake David made. TALK ABOUT MESSY.

Amon "did evil in the eyes of the Lord" and was assassinated after ruling for just two years. [1]

Then there was a season of Jews being exiled to Babylon. To put the cherry on top, Mary, who we know as the mother of Jesus, conceived by the Holy Spirit before her and Joseph were married. Try explaining that one to dad.

Today's devo is a little study heavy because it's important to see how God's plans for redemption played out in unique and messy ways. As we wait on God's plans to unfold, it can be easy to get swept away in the negativity and chaos that unfolds in our world.

Often times, we may not physically see God's hand at work, but we have generations of truth pointing us to a God who works despite our flaws, shortcomings, and pasts.

When the process is unfolding, we should be focused on the heart and hand of God, based on the promises He has held fast to and the ways He has shown up previously, whether we realize it or not. Trust is the first step in seasons of waiting, and God is inviting you into a season of remembrance. Remember how He has worked in your life previously. Remember the ways He was present for your friends or family. And if nothing comes to mind there, look to the truth of His Word and remember the ways He moved through generations of messiness, sin, angst, and pain to bring the greatest hope of Jesus into the world.

Reflect & Pray

What stories are you being reminded of that point you to God's presence and movement despite the mundane moments?

- leaving Willow by tough transition but finding peace & rest
- friendship - new & strong

What area is God asking you to trust in His promises a little bit more?

foster care
ministry work - career

Help. Thanks. Wow.

JESUS IS
timeless & thoughtful

December 4

History itself aligns with the promises and hope God lays out for His people.

Take a deep breath in and count to seven as you do. Deep breath out, count to seven. Seven in Hebrew is "sheba" which also means "promise, oath or covenant."[2] Seven is one of the most common numbers we see throughout Scripture, 735 times in fact.[3]

Looking at the genealogy yesterday, you might not have counted how many generations there were, but from the beginning of the promise to Abraham to the birth of Jesus, there are 42 generations.

"So all the generations from Abraham to David were fourteen generations, and from David to the deportation to Babylon fourteen generations, and from the deportation to Babylon to the Christ fourteen generations." Matthew 1:17

I don't know how long you've been holding onto a specific promise from God or what your waiting season has been like, but Abraham waited 42 generations to see the promise of his family line come to fruition in the arrival of Jesus Christ himself. The Israelites waited 400 years from the time the Prophets last spoke of the Messiah's coming to His actual arrival. Mary and Joseph waited 9 months to see how this crazy, unplanned pregnancy would unfold. Jesus waited about 33 years to fulfill His calling on earth which fulfilled the greatest promise of redemption for all of us waiting. If history reveals anything, it's that time *does* matter to God, and He recognizes how frustrating, devastating, and even sometimes boring the waiting can be. But what you'll see over the next couple of days is how He doesn't wait to move as we do; He works things out for our good in the meantime—we just often miss it when we're focused on the messiness instead.

Reflect & Pray

How long have you been waiting for something that makes it hard to be present in the moment?

3-4 years - calling, Kis' faith
1 month - K&K

As you reflect on a waiting season (or maybe one you're in right now), what do you notice about how God moves in the meantime, even when you might not see it immediately?

moves in ways I didn't know I needed.

What does the word "sheba" (promise, covenant, oath) mean to you as you wait?

It will come
or something better

Help. Thanks. Wow.

JESUS IS
making a way

December 5

Even in the messiest of situations, God makes a way.

"The word of the Lord came to Abram in a vision: 'Do not be afraid, Abram. I am your shield, your very great reward.' But Abram said, "Sovereign Lord, what can you give me since I remain childless... He took him outside and said, 'Look up at the sky and count the stars—if indeed you can count them.' Then he said to him, 'So shall your offspring be.' Abram believed the Lord, and he credited it to him as righteousness."
Genesis 15:1-2, 5

While Abram initially believed God's promise, things changed as time went on and the promise was not yet fulfilled. He and his wife, Sarai, decided to take matters into their own hands. Sarai and Abram chose to pursue an alternate form of offspring.

"But she had an Egyptian slave named Hagar; so she said to Abram, 'The Lord has kept me from having children. Go, sleep with my slave; perhaps I can build a family through her.'" Genesis 16:1-2

Sarai felt neglected by God since His promise hadn't been revealed in her expected timeline. Feel familiar? While that child, Ishmael, conceived by Hagar, is still a blessing, God had to remind Abram that His promise was greater than anything he and Sarai could perform on their own.

Speaking about Sarai, God said to Abram, "I will bless

her and will surely give you a son by her. I will bless her so that she will be the mother of nations; kings of peoples will come from her." Genesis 17:16

God shared a promise with Abram, a GREAT promise at that. Over time Abram and Sarai's doubt crept in, and they attempted to speed up the promise. *Has a sped-up promise ever been better than the original one God had in mind?* In God's graciousness, He didn't shun them for their choices. He made right the situation for Hagar (Genesis 16), and He reminded Abram and Sarai of His promise to them.

God's promises are never void of action, but His timing is often different than ours. While it wasn't wrong that Sarai and Abram doubted God's timing, their actions of defiance brought more weariness on them than if they had waited patiently. Nevertheless, God made a way through the mess to show them that He is still their "shield and very great reward." We must remember that letting go of our own processes allows God's plans to come through, so the promise is revealed when we need it most.

Reflect & Pray

What matter are you trying to take into your own hands as opposed to trusting God's promise is coming?

I feel good about waiting to do ministry but wonder if that is what God wants of me

Help. Thanks. Wow.

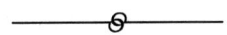

Verses to Remember

"But God shows his love for us in that while we were still sinners, Christ died for us."
Romans 5:8

"For by grace you have been saved through faith. And this is not your own doing; it is the gift of God, not a result of works, so that no one may boast. For we are his workmanship, created in Christ Jesus for good works, which God prepared beforehand, that we should walk in them."
Ephesians 2:8-10

"The steps of a man are established by the Lord, when he delights in his way; though he fall, he shall not be cast headlong, for the Lord upholds his hand."
Psalm 37:23-24

"But he said to me, 'My grace is sufficient for you, for my power is made perfect in weakness.' Therefore I will boast all the more gladly of my weaknesses, so that the power of Christ may rest upon me."
2 Corinthians 12:9

"The steadfast love of the Lord never ceases; his mercies never come to an end; they are new every morning; great is your faithfulness."
Lamentations 3:22-23

Jesus is more
than enough

JESUS IS
more than we imagine

December 6

Jesus offers more for us at our messiest than we would deserve even at our best.

"Therefore I tell you, do not be anxious about your life, what you will eat or what you will drink, nor about your body, what you will put on. Is not life more than food, and the body more than clothing? Look at the birds of the air: they neither sow nor reap nor gather into barns, and yet your heavenly Father feeds them. Are you not of more value than they? And which of you by being anxious can add a single hour to his span of life? And why are you anxious about clothing? Consider the lilies of the field, how they grow: they neither toil nor spin, yet I tell you, even Solomon in all his glory was not arrayed like one of these. But if God so clothes the grass of the field, which today is alive and tomorrow is thrown into the oven, will he not much more clothe you, O you of little faith?"
Matthew 6:25-30

It's important to recognize our messiness in order to appreciate God's expansive and incomprehensible grace and love, but we can't stay focused on the messiness forever. This Advent season, I believe God wants to remind you how much more valuable and precious you are in His sight than anything else. God is *more*, He has created you for *more*, and He offers *more* than you need. So what is it that you are having a hard time moving past in your messiness?

Whatever your anxieties, God offers you more peace.
Whatever your pain, God offers you more meaning.
Whatever your trials, God offers you more joy.
Whatever your joys, God offers you more hope.
Whatever your setbacks, God offers you more setup for something greater.
Whatever your fears, God offers you more steadfastness.
Whatever it is, God is more.

God is more, has more, offers more, created you for more, and prepares more than we can even understand. But that means we have to begin the process of laying down whatever is in the way of us experiencing the *more* He is offering. Jesus said it himself, He came to give us more and to be more for us so there would be a day with no more suffering and no more pain.

"The thief comes only to steal and kill and destroy. I came that they may have life and have it abundantly." John 10:10

Reflect & Pray

————— ☉ —————

What messiness in your life are you allowing to hold you back from experiencing *more* in Jesus Christ?

— pressed for time & too much activity makes me impatient & self-centred

Help. Thanks. Wow.

My fear —
that I'm done w/ministry
that I don't know how to
   lead W World / it will flop
that we won't have Katelynne
   Kaiden back w/us

JESUS IS
greater than all

December 7

What if you're so focused on the moments to come that you miss the more God is doing right now?

Now to him who is able to do far more abundantly than all that we ask or think, according to the power at work within us, to him be glory in the church and in Christ Jesus throughout all generations, forever and ever.
Ephesians 3:20-21

When Abraham and Sarah were anxiously awaiting their miracle pregnancy, it's obvious they wanted more. They couldn't wait for God's timing, so they tried to rush the process with their own plan. But God had something more for them on the other side.

When Mary and Joseph were navigating their unplanned pregnancy, they clearly (and understandably) wanted more. They wanted more explanation. Maybe they wanted more time to explain to friends and family, and I have to imagine they wanted more than an old, dirty, smelly animal stable. But somehow, in the mess, God had more for them than they could have asked or imagined.

When we think about our future and what we want in life, often we reflect that we want more (if we're really honest with ourselves). More time. More money. More friends. More opportunity. More chances. More space. More children.

Christmas manifests itself in America as a way to get and give more stuff. Not all of these are necessarily bad, but are they aligned with the *more* God might have in store for you?

Life is full of possibilities and great ones at that! God sees your heart, knows who He created you to be, and has a plan for you that is greater than you even know. Often, we're so focused on what we want more of in our future that we fail to see the more God is gifting us in our day-to-day lives. God's plan is always greater than our own, and while it's hard to surrender it to Him, it's so worth it in the end.

Reflect & Pray

When has God shown up in your life and done more than you expected?

Kindergarten job at transition
Love of Ronseth w/ fostering
Polar Express for kids
Joyce allowing us to visit

What is something you want more of that you need to surrender to Jesus, trusting His "more" is better?

Help. Thanks. Wow.

JESUS IS
unconditionally loving

December 8

Jesus came to remind us that He has more love for us than we ever thought possible, and more love than we can find anywhere else.

"So we have come to know and to believe the love that God has for us. God is love, and whoever abides in love abides in God, and God abides in him."
1 John 4:16

Think of the greatest act of love you've experienced. Remember the feeling? Like you belong, you're understood, someone finally sees you. Maybe you haven't felt a love like that, but you long for it. The kind of love God offers and extends to us is unmatched in all the world, but it is evident if we just lean in.

From the beginning of time, we see the world created out of God's unconditional love and built solely on relationships—the Trinity being the greatest relationship but also creating animals for humanity and woman for man. The Creator of our universe created life with the sole intent of being in relationship. Relationships are strongest when they are rooted in love, and with God, it is an unconditional love that can't be expressed in a single day of an Advent devotional.

While the greatest encouragement to understanding the kind of love God extends to us is to read through the story of Scripture in its entirety, I'll leave you with some examples to rest in as you dig into the kind of love you've seen throughout your life.

- God created humanity in His image to be in relationship with Him and each other (Genesis 2:18)
- God graciously communicates with His people daily (Psalm 145:18)
- God built covenants with us to establish trust and has never faltered (Isaiah 54:10)
- God's promises are always yes and amen (2 Corinthians 1:20)
- God's plans for us reveal a hope and future (Jeremiah 29:11)
- God sees us in our pain (Genesis 16)
- God sent His son to pay our debt to sin so we could be alive with Him forever (John 3:16)

God has been revealing His nature of love through creation, His promises, His presence, and His grace. Abiding in His love might mean reflecting on past moments that we overlooked. It might mean leaning into some of the pain we've experienced to see how He was comforting us through people, circumstances, or peace in moments of trial. It's learning to see His love in the present even when we struggle to see the light in our dark days.

Reflect & Pray

Where have you seen the thread of God's love be more than you ever thought possible? Do you need more of God's love today? What would that look like for you?

Help. Thanks. Wow.

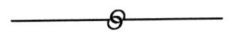

JESUS IS
our greatest hope

December 9

The first Christmas is a story of hope come to life, and that hope is still alive within us today.

"For God so loved the world, that he gave his only Son, that whoever believes in him should not perish but have eternal life."
John 3:16

It's often hard to see how there could possibly be a hope big enough to cover the weariness of our world. You may know this verse backward and forward. It may even feel over-simplified to you, but take a moment to re-read it, and consider what it really means for you, the hope you can carry with you each day.

We are sinners. It's a natural part of this broken world we live in, but God decided it wasn't good enough to have His beautiful creation pay the price for sin and forever be separated from His glory. Remember from yesterday, our God is a highly relational and loving God. He knew we needed more hope, so He reached down right where we are. He sent His son to be born in an old, smelly stable manger, and to live a life of perfection only to take the weight of our sins on the cross into death with Him. He did this so we could have eternal life—an eternity of painless, beautiful, peaceful, abundant joy. We will never have to struggle between the moments of sin, confession, forgiveness, and closeness to Him again because we will forever be with Him in Heaven.

This is the kind of hope our world needs, but it's so hard to see when our days are clouded with financial mishaps, devastating illness, and life-wrecking pain. Luckily, when we recognize the hope God offers, all that we face here on earth becomes more manageable, knowing that one day we will be freed from it all. It's hard to have a Heaven-perspective every day, but God reached down so we could have a little bit of Heaven, in the form of the Holy Spirit, within us. When we need more hope because things begin to look dreary and lost, we can ask the Spirit.

"For in this hope we were saved. But hope that is seen is no hope at all. Who hopes for what they already have? But if we hope for what we do not yet have, we wait for it patiently. In the same way, the Spirit helps us in our weakness. We do not know what we ought to pray for, but the Spirit himself intercedes for us through wordless groans." Romans 8:24-26

Reflect & Pray

What does it mean to you to have an eternal hope like this?

How does remembering this great hope help you as you navigate the frustrations you face in life?

Help. Thanks. Wow.

JESUS IS
good, all the time

December 10

Maybe in the waiting, God is revealing more time to pour into something we couldn't have before.

"I believe that I shall look upon the goodness of the Lord in the land of the living! Wait for the Lord; be strong, and let your heart take courage; wait for the Lord."
Psalm 27:13-14

We live in a culture that is always ready to jump to the next and greatest thing. Our patience and attention spans dip with every passing generation, and it shows in our spiritual lives if we're not careful to assess our hearts often. How many times have you said, "not enough hours in the day" when someone asks how you're doing? We often want more time, but when God gives it to us in a season of waiting for something better, we aren't sure what to do with it. *yes!*

When COVID-19 (coronavirus) hit the U.S. in March 2020, we were all given the blessing (though we definitely didn't see it as that at the time) of more time. While everyone handled quarantine differently, I took to my hobbies, and I was extremely energized with more time to write and pursue other fun projects.

Simultaneously, many have experienced much pain either personally or through other people's loss of jobs, sick family and friends, or just a general grief over what was going on in our world. Looking back, I was grateful that I not only had more time to explore new hobbies and rest, but we were all given a little bit more time to slow down and process what we were experiencing. It's something I'm sure many of us took for granted at times, but we have to remember that God's timing is always best.

What if, instead of complaining about waiting and being restless in the unknown, we took David's example from this Psalm and looked for God's goodness among our circumstances, with the extra time we're given while waiting? Maybe more time is what you're wanting right now or maybe it's the last thing you need. Wherever you are, recognize God's goodness in whatever He is giving you more of because His way is trustworthy and always works out to be exactly what our hearts, souls, and lives needed.

Reflect & Pray

What would you do if you were given more time right now? Do you feel like you have too much time on your hands?

How can you begin to see goodness in the gift of more time and take advantage of it you while you wait?

Help. Thanks. Wow.

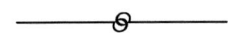

JESUS IS
full of opportunities

December 11

Don't let your discomfort get in the way of God's divine opportunities for you because you're too focused on your own plan.

"And he came to her and said, 'Greetings, O favored one, the Lord is with you!' But she was greatly troubled at the saying, and tried to discern what sort of greeting this might be. And the angel said to her, 'Do not be afraid, Mary, for you have found favor with God.'"
Luke 1:28-30

We don't know much about Mary before she conceived Jesus, but we do know she had her own plans. She was betrothed to Joseph, and she had a friend named Elizabeth (whom she visited after she received news of her own pregnancy). When Mary was visited by Gabriel, the angel, she wasn't sure what it meant. She tried to discern for herself what was happening before Gabriel reassured her. These moments come often in our lives —we're going about our business just as we had planned when God drops something unexpected in our laps.

Mary accepted the opportunity with an openness that most of us don't come by naturally. Her expression was confusion at first, to which she asked some clarifying questions (always a good idea when making a decision), but ultimately, she knew her trust in God was above all else. She welcomed the unprecedented opportunity because she trusted God to guide her in ways she didn't know she needed.

We often want more opportunities, but when greeted with them, we aren't convinced they're the "right" ones. What if, as this year comes to an end and a new year begins, you began to greet every opportunity (that aligns with Scripture) as God greeting you with a blessing because you have found favor in His eyes? Even when they sound uncomfortable, not because you have to accept all of them, but because you begin to trust that God's sovereignty is behind every opportunity, and He is looking out for your best.

Reflect & Pray

What more opportunities are you looking for in your life or what opportunities do you have in front of you that you are considering?

Who are your people to process divine opportunities with, in order to make the best decision according to where God is leading you?

Help. Thanks. Wow.

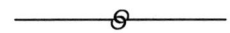

JESUS IS
all we need

December 12

When we seek more of God, He gives us more of everything we need.

"But seek first the kingdom of God and his righteousness, and all these things will be added to you."
Matthew 6:33

It's a natural human desire to want to ask for more things daily. I've grown to see it as a beautiful trait because it reveals something deep about the way God created us—we were made for more than this world has to offer. Naturally, we continue to strive for what "more" will fill our cups, but as you may know, nothing we can find here will satisfy. When God promises "more than we could ask or imagine," we tend to think it has to do with fulfilling earthly needs, but the closer we grow to Him, the more we begin to understand that it is beyond our experience on this earth.

It sounds trite, but that's only because we've made it that way in our culture. God really is more than enough for us, and when we seek *more of Him*, everything else falls into place as it's meant to be (not as we want it to be always). In order to live the most abundant life, we are to recognize God's place in the order of our priorities to ensure He is first. What that looks like on a daily basis will be different for all of us. When we lean into more of God, the natural response is for ourselves to become less, and this is an important part of surrendering daily that leads us to the greater life God has in store for us.

"He must increase, but I must decrease." John 3:30

There came a point, early on in humanity, that we realized we were nothing without God. Even then, we continued to search for more. As you read throughout Scripture, we see so many examples, time and time again, where people of God were seeking something more because they never felt like they had what they needed. Only when God showed up to reveal what they actually needed were they relieved of their need for more. So we struggle in this tension again and again in our time on earth, but when we look to God for more, He never disappoints as the world does.

Reflect & Pray

What does it look like for you to daily seek God more than you seek other things of this world?

How has God been enough for you in seasons where you were lacking?

Help. Thanks. Wow.

JESUS IS
our helper

December 13

Because of who Jesus Christ revealed Himself to be, you have more within you than you often give yourself credit for.

"So God created man in his own image, in the image of God he created him; male and female he created them."
Genesis 1:27

"But the Helper, the Holy Spirit, whom the Father will send in my name, he will teach you all things and bring to your remembrance all that I have said to you."
John 14:26

Right from the beginning of time, you can see that you are special. Not only did God create you as the completion of creation, but He did so by creating you in His own likeness. That doesn't mean you physically look like God or that you are God, but it means that His character is a part of who you are. Understanding more about God's character reveals more about ourselves, and that's when we begin to see His purposes for our lives unfold.

We had limited access to God throughout the days of the Old Testament which made Jesus' arrival *that much more* powerful. Jesus met us where we were in order to reveal to us more about Himself so we could be in relationship with Him. And that was just the beginning. As Jesus discussed life with His disciples, He mentioned the arrival of the third person of the Trinity—the Holy Spirit. Not only are we created in the likeness of God and His character, all believers now have the power and guidance of the Holy Spirit living within our hearts. This kind of relationship with God is like no other, and what it reveals to us is not just a deep connection to our Creator, but also a truth about how He can use us in furthering His Kingdom on earth. Because God lives within us, we have the strength to pursue whatever it is He puts before us—we just need to remember whose and who we are first.

Reflect & Pray

What is something unique God is revealing in you that is more than you saw in yourself before?

How can you cultivate the power of the Holy Spirit within you in order to move forward in the purposes set before you?

Help. Thanks. Wow.

More than Enough: Verses to Remember

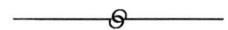

"The thief comes only to steal and kill and destroy. I came that they may have life and have it abundantly."
John 10:10

"Now to him who is able to do far more abundantly than all that we ask or think, according to the power at work within us, to him be glory in the church and in Christ Jesus throughout all generations, forever and ever. Amen."
Ephesians 3:20-21

"Abide in me, and I in you. As the branch cannot bear fruit by itself, unless it abides in the vine, neither can you, unless you abide in me. I am the vine; you are the branches. Whoever abides in me and I in him, he it is that bears much fruit, for apart from me you can do nothing."
John 15:4-5

"Have I not commanded you? Be strong and courageous. Do not be frightened, and do not be dismayed, for the Lord your God is with you wherever you go."
Joshua 1:9

JESUS IS
Immanuel

December 14

It's explicit in His name, Immanuel, that Jesus will never leave us, and that's not just a promise proclaimed, but a long-ago promise fulfilled.

"Fear not, for I am with you;
be not dismayed, for I am your God;
I will strengthen you, I will help you,
I will uphold you with my righteous right hand."
Isaiah 41:10

As we read the truth of God's story, we see the thread of His presence constantly—with the Israelites in their darkest hours, as they were slaves in Egypt, when they finally reached the promised land, and throughout the descendants of Abraham to the birth of Jesus. Jesus coming to earth as a baby was the greatest sign God could give that He would always be with us. It's the long-awaited sign we've needed since the moment Adam and Eve were sent out of the garden, and the beginning of waiting for Jesus' second arrival so we can all be at peace with God in Heaven. The birth of Jesus at the first Christmas revealed that there is deep meaning in God's presence, and His presence never leaves us.

"'She will bear a son, and you shall call his name Jesus, for he will save his people from their sins.' All this took place to fulfill what the Lord had spoken by the prophet: 'Behold, the virgin shall conceive and bear a son, and they shall call his name Immanuel' (which means, God with us)." Matthew 1:21-23

When the angel revealed the promised child to Joseph, he proclaimed that they name Him Jesus, which means "Yahweh is salvation" to fulfill the prophecy that Isaiah spoke. While Jesus and Immanuel (both names given to Jesus Christ) have different meanings, it can be understood that Jesus implies *what* He will do (save us) and Immanuel implies *how* He will do it (by our sides).[4]

Often we aren't paying enough attention to see God's presence with us in every moment, but that doesn't mean He isn't there. Jesus came to walk life with us on earth to reveal His deepest desire of presence with His people, and He didn't leave us alone when He ascended back into Heaven. This promise of His presence brings meaning to our everyday lives, but especially in this Advent season as we reflect on the greatest gift we ever received.

Reflect & Pray

When you recognize God's presence, what do you feel? How are you inclined to respond?

What does it mean to you that Jesus is our salvation and He is God with us in every moment?

Help. Thanks. Wow.

JESUS IS
a promise keeper

December 15

The waiting is not wasted time—it's where we see God's promises unfold before the plans take place.

"For I know the plans I have for you, declares the Lord, plans for welfare and not for evil, to give you a future and a hope. Then you will call upon me and come and pray to me, and I will hear you. You will seek me and find me, when you seek me with all your heart."
Jeremiah 29:11-13

We often know the first part of this Scripture, that God has plans for us, to bring us peace, a future, and hope. We lean into that, thinking that's the big promise here, but His promise is so much greater than the result of our waiting. His promise is that He will hear us when we call to Him, and we will find Him when we seek Him fully. Not only does He deliver a future of peace and hope, but He does so without leaving our side. He is always there when we need Him.

Waiting seasons can bring many different emotions. Fear, doubt, pain, weariness, hopelessness, loneliness, frustration, just to name a few. Have you felt any of those lately? Are you getting tired of just waiting for the promise to "arrive"? God's promise to us isn't waiting for arrival; it's here with us in the meantime. While the specific plan might not all play out at the exact time you thought, the promise of His presence brings meaning to your everyday life even while you wait.

As Mary waited to meet her unexpected baby boy, there were most likely some, if not all, of those emotions listed. As the Israelites waited for their time in the Promised Land, we see many of those emotions played out in their attitudes and actions. God doesn't give us seasons of waiting to torture or taunt us. He allows us seasons of space to recognize His presence and the promise of so much more than just what's at the end of waiting. If we never had to wait on His timing, we'd miss out on the meaning He reveals as we faithfully commit to showing up in the in-between seasons.

Reflect & Pray

What's one emotion you feel in your own season of waiting right now, even if it's just waiting for Christmas or the new year?

What can you do to actively recognize God's presence as part of the promise while you wait?

Help. Thanks. Wow.

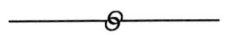

JESUS IS
always working

December 16

Even when it feels like God is not working, there is meaning for us in the silence.

"But when the set time had fully come, God sent his Son, born of a woman, born under the law."
Galatians 4:4

Even in silence, God is not absent. Quite the opposite, He is always present. From the last words of Malachi to the welcome news of Jesus' birth, there were 400 years of silence for the people of God. 400 years with no prophets, no miraculous and obvious acts of God, no Messiah, nothing. Though He may not have been as active in people's lives from their perspective, He was preparing for the greatest debut of all time.

Hindsight is always 20-20, and when we're in a season where we may not hear God frequently, it can feel as though He's no longer there and no longer cares. But His timing is greater than our own expectations, just as He sent Jesus at the perfect time. While it may have been painful for the people in that time period to not hear from God or actively see Him moving in their lives, it wasn't done in vain because God was still working. God knows best, and that includes His timing down to the very last millisecond.

What happened in the 400 years of silence set the stage for Jesus to enter at a time of relative peace, better transportation, and a common language throughout the Eastern World.[5] What's happening in your life during a time of silence could set the stage for God to reveal something even greater, but trusting His timing is key. Think of the truth of God's movement in your life. Even when you don't see it, He is working things out "for the good of those who love Him." (Romans 8:28)

Reflect & Pray

How has God surprised you in seasons of silence?

Where has your timing not aligned with God's plans for your life? Has that been frustrating? Is there a timing you're holding onto tightly that God might be asking you to release into His hands?

Help. Thanks. Wow.

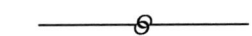

JESUS IS
preparing for us

December 17

You don't have to wait for the outcome to see meaning in the preparations.

"Now may the God of peace who brought again from the dead our Lord Jesus, the great shepherd of the sheep, by the blood of the eternal covenant, equip you with everything good that you may do his will, working in us that which is pleasing in his sight, through Jesus Christ."
Hebrews 13:20-21

We spend many hours preparing for the holiday, for dinner with family, parties, gifts, gatherings. Just like you prepare for these events, God is asking you to prepare your heart and life for His presence, and specifically for His return. While Mary and Joseph were awaiting the arrival of not just their baby, but the Son of God, they prepared. They followed the orders to go back to their birthplace for the census, and they searched high and low for a place to lay their heads to be ready for Jesus' arrival.

The entire Old Testament tells of centuries of preparation for Jesus' birth, life, death, resurrection, and reconciliation with His people. It's the greatest setup of all time, and we tend to overlook the setup God might be doing in our own lives because we're too focused on the goal. If Jesus was only thinking about the end-game, how different do you think His ministry and life would have been? His entire life on earth exemplified how we ought to conduct ourselves in the "meantime" moments of life, while we're preparing for what God has ahead for us.

Faith in God takes precedence, but faith should always ignite action, and that's where preparation begins. God is equipping you right now for something you may not even know about yet, and He is simply asking you to act in faith and begin to prepare for what He might have in store for you.

Reflect & Pray

How can you be preparing right now for something God might have in store for your future?

What does it look like to find joy in the preparations?

Help. Thanks. Wow.

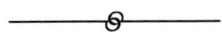

JESUS IS
my shepherd

December 18

Your circumstances do not define or diminish God's presence.

"The Lord is my shepherd; I shall not want.
He makes me lie down in green pastures.
He leads me beside still waters.
He restores my soul. He leads me in paths of righteousness for his name's sake.
Even though I walk through the valley of the shadow of death, I will fear no evil,
for you are with me;
your rod and your staff, they comfort me.
You prepare a table before me in the presence of my enemies; you anoint my head with oil; my cup overflows.
Surely goodness and mercy shall follow me all the days of my life,
and I shall dwell in the house of the Lord forever."
Psalm 23

This Psalm is remarkable, and you have probably heard it before. What is so present in this truth is that God is always with us, guiding us, giving us rest, protecting us, comforting us, preparing us, defending us, anointing us, and giving us far more than we deserve. In every scenario listed here which covers any scenario you may find yourself in, God *is* there.

Filled with joy as you rest? God is smiling with you.

Fearful as you walk through dark circumstances? God is holding your hand, protecting you.

Unsettled in your soul as the world grows in chaos? God is leading you to a place of restoration.

Not sure what direction to go in life? God is right there, guiding you on paths of righteousness.

Wherever you're at in life, whatever you're facing, know today that you're not facing it alone. God is omnipresent. He goes before you to prepare the way, walks with you to comfort and guide you, and protects behind you so nothing can truly harm you. While you will face trials and hardship, they are temporary, but God's protection, love, and plan is eternal.

Reflect & Pray

What circumstances feel bigger than God's presence right now?

What from this Psalm do you need most right now from God's presence? Guidance? Protection? Restoration? Preparation? Goodness? Mercy? Ask Him for it today, and trust that He is *for* you.

Help. Thanks. Wow.

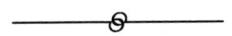

JESUS IS
victorious over all

December 19

*The glory that is to come is far greater
than our present sufferings.*

"For I consider that the sufferings of this present time
are not worth comparing with the glory that is to be
revealed to us. For the creation waits with eager
longing for the revealing of the sons of God."
Romans 8:18-19

What was your day like yesterday? What setbacks did
you face and how did your expectations get thwarted?
How about this week? This last year? The truth is that
our expectations will never measure up to what God
truly intends for us to experience, but we get focused on
what we thought the plan should be, and we leave no
space for growth and deeper faith. Paul, who wrote the
book of Romans, suffered immensely, and he wrote this
truth with such confidence because he knew that
whatever God had for him would be worth the suffering
he endured.

Maybe this year has brought you a lot of suffering or
confusion, change or instability. Christmas tends to
exacerbate those emotions with the pressure of the
season, but what if this year could be different? What if
you found meaning in your suffering?

Jesus never promised an easy life without pain, but He
promised a path that leads to the greatest reward and a
life of peace with Him. No matter what circumstances

you may face, God is there with you. Even now, the reminder for today is that what God has in store for you is far greater than anything you could hope to experience on this earth. If you're having a hard time holding onto hope in the promise of tomorrow because the suffering of today is too great, write these truths down somewhere you'll see them often.

The glory God will reveal . . .

- Can never be taken away (Romans 8:39)
- Is victorious over all (Deuteronomy 20:4)
- Means death to death, and life for me (Romans 8:1-2)
- Restores hope and exuberant joy within us (Romans 5:1-2)

Reflect & Pray

Which of the attributes of God's glory do you need most right now?

Are you able to find meaning in your suffering right now? It's okay if not—just make that your prayer today, that God would reveal His glory through your pain.

Help. Thanks. Wow.

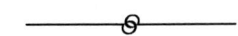

# JESUS IS
relational

December 20

*People are often our greatest gauge for
our proximity to Jesus.*

"John answered them all, saying, "I baptize you with
water, but he who is mightier than I is coming, the
strap of whose sandals I am not worthy to untie. He will
baptize you with the Holy Spirit and fire."
Luke 3:16

The relationships we build and company we keep are a
great representation of how we choose to live our lives,
what is most important to us, and where we place
God. When we start to make snap judgments of
others, and if we begin to isolate or react poorly in
conversations, it's a good time to take a quick
evaluation of our heart and how often we're spending
time with God.

John the Baptist, Elizabeth's son born shortly before
Jesus, was called to prepare people for Jesus' arrival
and ministry. He was the first voice to speak of the
Messiah's coming since the 400-year silence from the
Old Testament prophets. He began to remind people
that there was greater meaning in their lives that was
about to be revealed.

Finding meaning in our everyday lives becomes easier
when we surround ourselves with those pointing us to
Jesus. Without those sound voices, we can find
ourselves outside the will of God and losing ourselves

because of our instinctual nature as humans to wander. God created a need for relationships at our core for this very reason.

While it may look different for everyone, one thing crucial to our faith journey is a community of believers we can walk through life with. You know that saying, if you want to know a person's character, just look at their friends. While this can be nuanced, there's a lot of value in who you spend your time with regularly, and God wants to show you meaning in your life through the people you interact with.

Reflect & Pray

Who in your life is pointing you to Jesus the way John did? Who are you pointing to Jesus in the same way?

What's the greatest value your community has brought you this year? If you haven't found solid community, what are you looking for in a friend?

Help. Thanks. Wow.

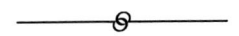

Meaning in Every Moment: Verses to Remember

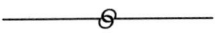

"And we know that for those who love God all things work together for good, for those who are called according to his purpose."
Romans 8:28

"Do not be anxious about anything, but in everything by prayer and supplication with thanksgiving let your requests be made known to God. And the peace of God, which surpasses all understanding, will guard your hearts and your minds in Christ Jesus."
Philippians 4:6-7

"Looking to Jesus, the founder and perfecter of our faith, who for the joy that was set before him endured the cross, despising the shame, and is seated at the right hand of the throne of God. Consider him who endured from sinners such hostility against himself, so that you may not grow weary or fainthearted."
Hebrews 12:2-3

"I know how to be brought low, and I know how to abound. In any and every circumstance, I have learned the secret of facing plenty and hunger, abundance and need."
Philippians 4:12

miracles
in the meantime

JESUS IS
sovereign & divine

December 21

Even unexpected and unwanted miracles are a revelation of God's divine hand at work in our lives because of His great love for us.

"For my thoughts are not your thoughts, neither are your ways my ways, declares the Lord. For as the heavens are higher than the earth, so are my ways higher than your ways and my thoughts higher than your thoughts."
Isaiah 55:8-9

Mary's pregnancy was not only unplanned, it was completely unprecedented and most likely unwanted (at least at the time, given the circumstances of her pending wedding). But it was still a wonderful miracle! When you hear the word miracle, what do you think of? Jesus turning water into wine? Mary conceiving a child as a virgin? Jesus healing a lame man? A woman who had been bleeding for 12 years healed immediately simply by a touch of Jesus' robe? These miracles seem out of reach in our context, as if God no longer performs miracles to reveal His caring and all-powerful nature, but He does.

Miracles come in all shapes and sizes, and even when we don't see it, God is working in every area of our lives to reveal His strength and goodness. We may not recognize the miracles often because we don't think or live even remotely similar to how God does. He is so far above what we can comprehend that it's hard to wrap our mind around the idea of miracles in our own lives. When a curveball gets thrown our way, we often see it as an obstacle instead of an opportunity, a mess instead of a potential miracle.

As you anticipate this upcoming season, and maybe the arrival of a specific promise, the closer you get to God, the more He will open your eyes to see possibilities in the problems and miracles in the meantime.

Reflect & Pray

Where do you need a miracle in your life right now?

Is there a problem or obstacle you're facing that God might be able to turn into a miraculous opportunity?

Have you seen God reveal Himself through miracles (maybe relationships being mended or financial blessing) in your life? What was that experience like, and how does that give you hope for your future?

Help. Thanks. Wow.

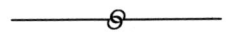

JESUS IS
a miracle worker

December 22

May we begin to feel the weight of God's glory, grace, and hope more than the weight of our sorrows, failures, and weariness.

"For to us a child is born, to us a son is given; and the government shall be upon his shoulder, and his name shall be called Wonderful Counselor, Mighty God, Everlasting Father, Prince of Peace. Of the increase of his government and of peace there will be no end, on the throne of David and over his kingdom, to establish it and to uphold it with justice and with righteousness from this time forth and forevermore."
Isaiah 9:6-7

Isaiah's prophecy was fulfilled the day Mary gave birth to Jesus, and the world finally understood what they had waited for. The miracle of this birth is a small part of the greater miracle in God's redemption of humanity, but it's all important to even our lives now. If He really is all He says He is and Isaiah prophesied Him to be here, then our lives should reflect that.

It's okay to not be okay, but it's not okay to stay there because a life of following Christ is a life of trusting in something far greater than your circumstances and sorrows. It means trusting that our failures don't change our future and our weakness paves a way for God's strength to carry us even further. Following Jesus reminds us that He is Lord over all, including that which we have no control over. We remember that He can and will bring peace and hope to people and lands that are in deep need of saving and redemption - that's the greatest miracle we can experience in our lifetime.

The miracle God may be hoping to reveal in your life is that He is working behind the scenes or that you will be able to release the burden of your pain and instead receive the light yoke of His goodness and grace. May this Christmas be the Advent of peace where there was pain and hope where there was hurt. May this be the year that your favorite gift is receiving God's love in a way that gives you freedom and life.

Reflect & Pray

What sorrow or pain is weighing you down this season?

How can you release that burden to allow God to reveal His glory to you this year?

Help. Thanks. Wow.

JESUS IS
Prince of Peace

December 23

While you wait, begin to recognize the little miracles around you every day and watch your weary anticipation turn to recollection of God's goodness.

"Enter his gates with thanksgiving, and his courts with praise! Give thanks to him; bless his name! For the Lord is good; his steadfast love endures forever, and his faithfulness to all generations."
Psalm 100:4-5

Many times we neglect to see the miracles God is performing in our lives because we don't take the time to recognize and thank Him for everything He is for us. As we consider His presence, we are filled with awe of all He has done and is doing, especially throughout the ages. He is faithful. He is righteous. He is just. He is considerate and caring. He fights for us. He pursues us. Even when we're overwhelmed with anxiety and pain, He is our comforter, our Prince of Peace.

As we head into the final days of Christmas, what are you thankful for? Who has God been for you? Take some extra time to list out your gratitude and begin to replace a worry a day with a moment of thanks. See how it transforms your thought life and allows you space to recognize the little miracles of everyday.

Reflect & Pray

Where are you recognizing the little or big miracles throughout your days? What are you thankful for in this moment that you may easily overlook?

We talk a lot about being thankful this time of year, but how could you make it a daily habit?

Who are you grateful for right now? Take time to send them a message or give them a call to let them know how much they mean to you!

Help. Thanks. Wow.

JESUS IS
trustworthy

December 24

When God only gives us glimpses of the promise, it's an invitation to trust Him with the journey.

"Blessed is the one who trusts in the Lord,
whose trust is the Lord."
Jeremiah 17:7

Can you imagine how Mary felt? Having just ridden on a donkey for days, getting rejected everywhere they sought shelter, and realizing that soon, she was going to birth not just a child, not just her first child, but the Son of God. The eve of Christ's birth must have been stressful, finding the only place to lay their head among the animals in the stable and not even understanding the full picture of what Jesus would be like or what He was meant to do on earth. I'm sure you can relate to that feeling.

Often, God just gives us glimpses of the full picture. He doesn't do so as a way to tease and torture us, but rather to invite us to trust the process in His hands. Before Mary saw the ultimate beauty of Jesus' story play out, she was most likely overwhelmed with fear, shame, a burden of responsibility. Yet, she trusted. Not that she always thought things were perfect and wonderful, as I'm sure there were many not-easy moments in those first 9 months, and we know from Scripture that Jesus wasn't always the easiest child (He left Mary and Joseph in the marketplace to go to the temple, for example). But even in the midst of the worry and stress, Mary chose to trust God's process.

Today, the eve before Christmas, we're reflecting on the miracle of trusting God in the process. As you hurry to get your plans ready for your holiday festivities, bring God into the planning with you. As you begin to feel burdened with all that's going on, remember that God is in control, and let Him share the load. God is calling you to rest in His presence, not just when you're on vacation, but as a daily practice. Even in the hustle and bustle of the Christmas season, there can be rest found in Jesus when you trust His process over yours.

Reflect & Pray

How can you invite God into your preparations today so you keep Him as the main focus of the holiday?

What part of the journey with God are you really enjoying right now that is life-giving and energizing? How are you staying encouraged in your faith?

Help. Thanks. Wow.

JESUS IS
our Savior

December 25

The miracle of Christmas should never be overlooked as simple or outdated as it is the heartbeat of the hope we have in our relationship with the Savior of the world, born that very day.

"And suddenly there was with the angel a multitude of the heavenly host praising God and saying, 'Glory to God in the highest, and on earth peace among those with whom he is pleased!'"
Luke 2:13-14

Looking for a miracle, for meaning, for more than your current circumstances? God graced us with all that and more when Mary welcomed her sweet babe into the world. We no longer have to wonder IF things will get better or IF we'll be redeemed. We are, and things will.

Our hope began when Jesus was born because His life is the representation of Immanuel, God with us. Isn't that worth celebrating today? Before you rush into the presents under the tree and the cinnamon rolls in the oven, take a moment to sit in the awe of this day.

"O Holy Night" is a beautiful song, reminding us of God's hope, peace, love, and joy. One of the most prominent lines declares,

"His law is love, and His gospel is peace."

If you have time, listen to the song and really lean into the words. When Jesus came into this world, He didn't abolish the law—He fulfilled it with something far greater, *love*. He brought peace to a world that fought over trivial matters, and His response to injustice, war, financial woes, and pain was love. When you need hope, look to the truth of who God is because love is our greatest hope of all.

Love is the hope this weary world needs more than anything else. Love is the backbone for dreams of peace. Love is the foundation for true joy. God's love covers all indecency, all sin, all failures, all rejection, all suffering, all fear, and all uncertainty. All you have to do is receive that love that came down to be with us on that first Christmas day and chose to stay forever.

Reflect & Pray

How is God in your midst this Christmas morning?

Will you simply receive the greatest gift of love today from your Heavenly Father who looks down on you and calls you "beloved"?

Help. Thanks. Wow.

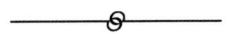

Miracles in the Meantime: Verses to Remember

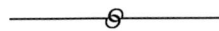

"And the Word became flesh and dwelt among us, and we have seen his glory, glory as of the only Son from the Father, full of grace and truth."
John 1:14

"But Jesus looked at them and said, 'With man this is impossible, but with God all things are possible.'"
Matthew 19:26

"He said to them, 'Because of your little faith. For truly, I say to you, if you have faith like a grain of mustard seed, you will say to this mountain, 'Move from here to there,' and it will move, and nothing will be impossible for you."
Matthew 17:20

"'Truly, truly, I say to you, whoever believes in me will also do the works that I do; and greater works than these will he do, because I am going to the Father.'"
John 14:12

"You are the God who works wonders; you have made known your might among the peoples."
Psalm 77:14

moving
into God's calling

JESUS IS
always faithful

December 26

Is God's faithfulness in your past enough to motivate you forward in what He is calling you to?

"He who calls you is faithful; he will surely do it."
1 Thessalonians 5:24

As you head into the last few days of this year, you'll have time to process how God is moving you forward. Look back on some of the reflections from the last 25 days. We remembered the messiness of this broken world and how God meets us there. We reflected on God being more than enough for us, and how He is continuously working miracles when we least expect it. The miracle of Jesus Himself being the greatest of all.

The point of reflecting on miracles in the meantime is that we will be forever transformed and that our lives would reflect that transformation. Now is the time to move into the space God has curated for you. Now is the time to move into a season of actively seeking God daily and seeing His movement because of your closeness to Him. Now is the time to *move* as He calls you, trusting His faithfulness in the process.

As you plan for the upcoming year, it's easy to get caught up thinking through all the ways you should be faithful to God. We often put the burdens of our responsibilities so heavy on our own shoulders that we forget it's God's faithfulness to us that should be carrying the weight. If we're not trusting in His faithfulness, how can we truly expect to be faithful to Him in the long-run? Why would we remain faithful to someone we don't fully trust?

"The saying is trustworthy, for if we have died with him, we will also live with him; if we endure, we will also reign with him; if we deny him, he also will deny us; if we are faithless, he remains faithful—for he cannot deny himself." 2 Timothy 2:11-13

When we give it all to God because of what He gave for us, we gain everything we need. Let this be your reminder as you consider how He's asking you to act in faith this year. His faithfulness to you is what will carry the weight of your responsibilities in righteous and faithfulness to Him.

Reflect & Pray

How did your Christmas holiday meet or not meet your expectations?

What is God asking you to be faithful to as you move into this next year?

Help. Thanks. Wow.

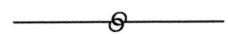

JESUS IS
our anchor

December 27

Let the assuredness of God's promise be the very thing that lifts your spirit every morning to keep moving forward with the very things He asks you to do, for His glory.

"We have this as a sure and steadfast anchor of the soul, a hope that enters into the inner place behind the curtain, where Jesus has gone as a forerunner on our behalf, having become a high priest forever."
Hebrews 6:19-20

We've talked a lot about God's promises this season, but it's something God is constantly calling us to look back on because we too quickly forget to trust Him. The author of Hebrews reflected on the promise God made to Abraham, and reminds us that God makes oaths with His children as a way to share "strong encouragement to hold fast to the hope set before us." (Hebrews 6:18) What is the hope set before us?

The hope we seek is the hope of God's promises fulfilled. We see the fruit of His promises all throughout history, and especially in the story of the birth of Jesus Christ. Christ is the hope set before us, and He is now the hope that keeps us moving forward. While our faith is built on things unseen, there is an assurance in the stories, in the Word of God as revealed through Scripture, and in the promise of His life, death, and resurrection. The hope we have in Christ Is to be with

Him forever, seated at the right hand of the Father. This is more than a simple hope; we can be confident in that because of how He has moved on our behalf.

In Hebrews 6, the author highlights Abraham as an example of faith and patience, and that in itself should be enough hope to motivate you. Abraham wasn't perfect, but He walked closer with God every day which brought Him eventually to the revelation of the promise to be a father to many nations. So the promise was fulfilled, not because he was was perfect at waiting or that it happened in his timing, but because God is a faithful God, and Abraham stayed faithful in response.

Reflect & Pray

Do you have assuredness of hope today in God's ultimate plan? If yes, how does that encourage you practically? If no, what do you need from God to have this level of confidence?

Help. Thanks. Wow.

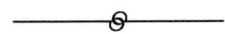

JESUS IS
our source of life

December 28

In order to take strides in our life and faith, we are called to abide in Jesus as He abides in us.

"I am the vine; you are the branches. Whoever abides in me and I in him, he it is that bears much fruit, for apart from me you can do nothing."
John 15:5

Jesus is to be apart of every aspect of our lives. When you start thinking through your future, how God wants to use you and move through you, the most important caveat is that He is the one leading the way.

The word abide means to remain, to dwell, to reside with. When we choose to abide in Jesus, we are committing to a life of dwelling in His presence. While that sounds like that would keep us still, it is the very thing that propels us to move as He designed so we aren't out of step with His plans for us. It all goes back to fully trusting in Him.

This verse highlights something special about our relationship with God in that when we abide in Him, He also abides in us. God chooses you. He chooses you everyday, and He patiently waits for you to choose Him. Because He abides in you, you don't have to wonder where He is or IF He is with you. He is. No question. When we abide, and He abides in return, we are able to do far more than we could on our own.

Moving into the place God has prepared for us means bearing fruit, being witnesses to others in this world, and sharing the good news of the Gospel with those who need it most. How can you expect to move well without remaining in Jesus daily? This is more than an invitation to be kept and protected by His presence— this is an expectation to draw near to Him so He can be the very thing pouring out of you.

Reflect & Pray

How are you abiding in Jesus daily? What does it mean to you that Jesus abides in you?

What fruit do you see in your life from abiding in Jesus?

Help. Thanks. Wow.

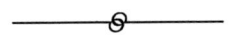

JESUS IS
unchanging

December 29

When your hope and trust is fully in Christ, you cannot be moved, regardless of what the world throws your way.

"I have set the LORD always before me: because he is at my right hand, I shall not be moved."
Psalm 16:8 (KJV)

As you begin to think about what this next year might look like for you, where is God?

While He is continually moving us forward, the best place we can move is closer to Him. Only there are we unshakable and steady in His arms. While movement is the natural next step after faith in God, it sometimes takes even more strength to not be moved when circumstances, worldly influences, and personal dreams fight to sway us.

Everything around you changes. You change. Your home may change. Your job may change. Your friendships may change. Politics, churches, and wars change. God never will.

"Jesus Christ is the same yesterday and today and forever." Hebrews 13:8

This promise is what grounds our faith in assurance

and strength. It's hard to fully grasp because of the uncertainty this world offers us daily, but when we study the truth of God's Word, we can see His unchanging hope, peace, love, and joy. That's what we're holding onto after this Advent season. While Jesus was the notable arrival back then, we're still waiting for His second arrival to redeem and renew the earth in its entirety.

In the meantime, we can be confident in three prominent truths:

- His Word is true, and it is the greatest tool at our disposal for remembering who He is, who He created us to be, and how we ought to move in response.
- His promises are never-failing, and His love is never ending for His children, even as flawed and messy as we are.
- Our hope remains confident because of His steadfastness and faithfulness to us throughout all time.

Reflect & Pray

How does the steadiness and unchanging truth of God bring peace to your preparations for the new year?

Help. Thanks. Wow.

JESUS IS
Wonderful Counselor

December 30

Invite God into your goal-setting plans for the new year, and watch as His vision expands your life more than you even thought possible.

Stereotypically, every year during this time, we are all hunkered down in our new year planners, vision-mapping our lives, and landing a "new year resolution." Those are great things, but where is God in the midst of it? God won't ask you about your weight loss or morning routine goals when you get to the gates. While these are good goals to think through as you consider how you'll accomplish His ultimate goals for you, what matters most is your proximity to God and proximity to His people.

"'And you shall love the Lord your God with all your heart and with all your soul and with all your mind and with all your strength.' The second is this: 'You shall love your neighbor as yourself.' There is no other commandment greater than these." Mark 12:30-31

In a leadership program I was a part of, we had a saying that would always reset our perspective (and give us a chuckle). Whenever things felt weary or draining (or weird and uncomfortable), we would simply say "#FORTHEKINGDOM." Whether we were setting up chairs, stepping on cockroaches during Fright Night in High School Ministry, or staying up all night to get ready for an outreach ministry, #forthekingdom. It helped us shift our attention from the nuisance of the task at hand to our *why* behind it—our goal was always to bring people closer to God and do what we could to further His Kingdom on earth.

Whatever you are doing to prepare for making this new year everything it can be and more, remember #forthekingdom and let God align your goals with His greater vision for your life. By the end of this devotional, I hope you can recognize His hand in your life so you can trust His guidance to move you in the right direction in His timing.

Reflect & Pray

What direction do you feel God nudging you in this next year, even if it's uncomfortable?

What is one goal you have for the new year?

What is your why (#forthekingdom) behind this goal? Write it down to reflect on when it's hard to follow through.

Help. Thanks. Wow.

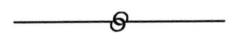

JESUS IS
always moving

December 31

If we schedule enough space in our calendar to slow down, we will see the goodness of God moving all around us.

"God is our refuge and strength,
a very present help in trouble.
Therefore we will not fear though the earth gives way,
though the mountains be moved into the heart of the sea,
though its waters roar and foam,
though the mountains tremble at its swelling.
There is a river whose streams make glad the city of God,
the holy habitation of the Most High.
God is in the midst of her; she shall not be moved;
God will help her when morning dawns.
The nations rage, the kingdoms totter;
he utters his voice, the earth melts;
The Lord of hosts is with us;
the God of Jacob is our fortress.
Come, behold the works of the Lord,
how he has brought desolations on the earth.
He makes wars cease to the end of the earth;
he breaks the bow and shatters the spear;
he burns the chariots with fire.
'Be still, and know that I am God.
I will be exalted among the nations,
I will be exalted in the earth!'
The Lord of hosts is with us;
the God of Jacob is our fortress."
Psalm 46

May this next year be more full of hope, peace, love, and joy despite the circumstances, storms, or celebrations you experience. God is always in your midst; it's your call to give Him the space in your life to *move*.

Reflect & Pray

What do you hope to see God do in the next 365 days?

Where do you see His presence active in your waiting season?

What "good news" did He reveal to you in the last 31 days or what good news are you still waiting on?

What's the greatest joy you are taking from this year with you into the next year?

Help. Thanks. Wow.

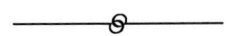

Move into God's Calling: Verses to Remember

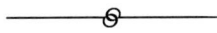

"And I am sure of this, that he who began a good work in you will bring it to completion at the day of Jesus Christ."
Philippians 1:6

"The LORD is near to all who call on him, to all who call on him in truth."
Psalm 145:18

"Seek the Lord while He may be found;
Call upon Him while He is near."
Isaiah 55:6

"Be still, and know that I am God.
I will be exalted among the nations,
I will be exalted in the earth!"
Psalm 46:10

"Therefore, brethren, be all the more diligent to make certain about His calling and choosing you; for as long as you practice these things, you will never stumble"
2 Peter 1:10

This is Just the Beginning

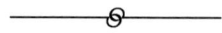

Mary believed greatly in the goodness of God, and she sang this song recorded in Luke 1:46-55 after sharing the news with her friend Elizabeth. As they joined together in the joy (and probably some fear) of their unexpected pregnancies, they rejoiced. As you enter a new year, hopefully more burden-free and peaceful than before, take these words of remembrance and gratitude with you every day.

"My soul magnifies the Lord,
and my spirit rejoices in God my Savior,
for he has looked on the humble estate of his servant.
For behold, from now on all generations will call
me blessed;
for he who is mighty has done great things for me,
and holy is his name.
And his mercy is for those who fear him
from generation to generation.
He has shown strength with his arm;
he has scattered the proud in the thoughts of
their hearts;
he has brought down the mighty from their thrones
and exalted those of humble estate;
he has filled the hungry with good things,
and the rich he has sent away empty.
He has helped his servant Israel,
in remembrance of his mercy,
as he spoke to our fathers,
to Abraham and to his offspring forever."

And blessed is she who believed
that there would be a fulfillment of
what was spoken to her from the Lord.

Luke 1:45

About the Author

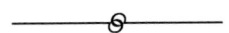

Stephanie was born and raised in a Christian home and has always been involved in church and school leadership. She developed a love for reading and writing at a young age, and has since been discovering God's call to write for others to grow closer to God daily. She graduated with a BA in English from William Jessup University and received her MA in Christian Ministry from North Park University. She hopes to use her degrees and experience to help further church communications strategies.

When she's not working in full-time ministry, Stephanie is likely writing, podcasting, knee deep in Enneagram Memes, or getting coffee with a friend (that is, when she's not curled up, watching a movie with her husband and small pup). As a self-proclaimed multi-passionate person, Stephanie loves the pursuit of new projects, new perspectives, and mapping out new plans. She consults, builds websites, designs book covers, and formats/edits books for fellow passionate bloggers and writers. Needless to say, busy is a well-used word in her vocabulary, but all for the glory of God.

Stephanie lives with her husband, Jared and their mini-bernadoodle, Hazel in Sacramento, California where the heat is nearly unbearable, but the access to all God's beautiful nature makes it worth it. You can find her creating new content and keeping up with the hustle of life online at www.stephanielapreal.com or on Instagram @stephlapreal and Twitter @stephlapreal_.

Bibliography

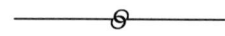

1 King Amon
https://www.gotquestions.org/King-Amon.html

2 The Number 7 Meaning
https://bibleresources.info/what-does-the-number-14-represent-in-the-bible-reference/

3 The Number 7 Usage
https://angelnumber.org/what-does-the-number-7-mean-in-the-bible/#:~:text=This%20number%20is%20mentioned%20735,sevenfold%E2%80%9C%20is%20used%206%20times.

4 Jesus and Immanuel Names
https://goexplorethebible.com/blog/adults/what-is-the-relationship-between-the-names-jesus-and-immanuel/

5 400 Years of Silence
https://www.mcall.com/entertainment/mc-fea-faith-eric-yeakel-god-silent-20171214-story.html

Made in the USA
Monee, IL
21 November 2021